D1568544

A Construction Worker's Tools

Jesse McFadden

PowerKiDS press.

New York

Published in 2016 by The Rosen Publishing Group, Inc.
29 East 21st Street, New York, NY 10010

First Edition

Editor: Caitie McAneney
Book Design: Reann Nye

Library of Congress Cataloging-in-Publication Data

McFadden, Jesse.
A construction worker's tools / by Jesse McFadden.
p. cm. — (Community helpers and their tools)
Includes index.
ISBN 978-1-4994-0836-2 (pbk.)
ISBN 978-1-4994-0837-9 (6 pack)
ISBN 978-1-4994-0890-4 (library binding)
1. Tools — Juvenile literature. 2. Building — Juvenile literature. 3. Construction workers — Juvenile literature. I. McFadden, Jesse. II. Title.
TJ1195.M356 2016
621.9—d23

Manufactured in the United States of America

CPSIA Compliance Information: Batch #WS15PK: For Further Information contact Rosen Publishing, New York, New York at 1-800-237-9932

Contents

Construction Tools

Do you like to build things? If you do, you might like a job as a construction worker. Construction workers are community helpers who construct, or build, houses, stores, bridges, and even roads.

Construction workers need a good team to get the job done. They also need many tools. They need small tools such as hammers and screwdrivers. They also need big tools such as trucks and cranes. A construction worker's job is sometimes unsafe. They have tools and clothing to **protect** them from harm.

Some construction workers get to drive big machines such as this bulldozer. A bulldozer is a tractor with a long blade for clearing objects and leveling the land.

What to Wear

Construction workers wear helmets, also called hard hats, to protect their head. This keeps them safe from objects that might fall at a construction **site**. Hard hats are often yellow. Many construction sites have signs that say "hard hat area" to remind people to protect their heads.

Construction workers often wear brightly colored vests. These vests help other people see construction workers. This is important because construction sites are often near roads where trucks and other cars speed by. The vests make workers more **visible** to drivers and other workers.

TOOL TIME!

Construction workers often wear safety glasses to protect their eyes.

safety glasses

steel toe boots

Construction workers wear heavy boots with steel in the toe. This keeps their feet safe from falling objects.

Small Tools

Construction workers use many small tools. A construction worker may use a hammer to drive a nail into wood. A hammer has a metal head and a handle. One side of the head is flat for driving the nail. The other side often has a claw for pulling nails out of wood.

Construction workers use screwdrivers to turn screws into wood. A screwdriver has a head and a handle. Flathead screwdrivers have a flat head, while Phillips screwdrivers have a cross-shaped head.

Nails and screws are tiny tools. They come in many shapes and sizes.

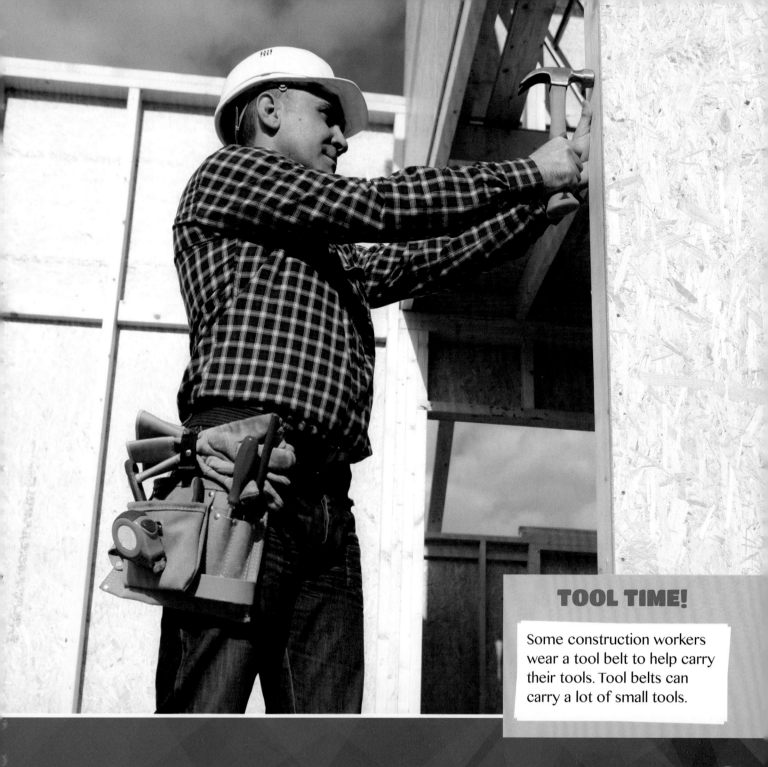

TOOL TIME!

Some construction workers wear a tool belt to help carry their tools. Tool belts can carry a lot of small tools.

Power Tools

Sometimes construction workers need to drive hundreds of nails a day. It would take a very long time to hammer those nails by hand. That's why many construction workers use power tools, which are powered by **sources** such as electricity.

A nail gun can drive thousands of nails a day! A construction worker only needs to press a button on the handle for a nail to shoot out. When screwdrivers take too long, a worker might use a drill. Power drills can turn screws quickly and easily.

drill

TOOL TIME!

Some drills have cords that connect to electrical outlets. Others use batteries.

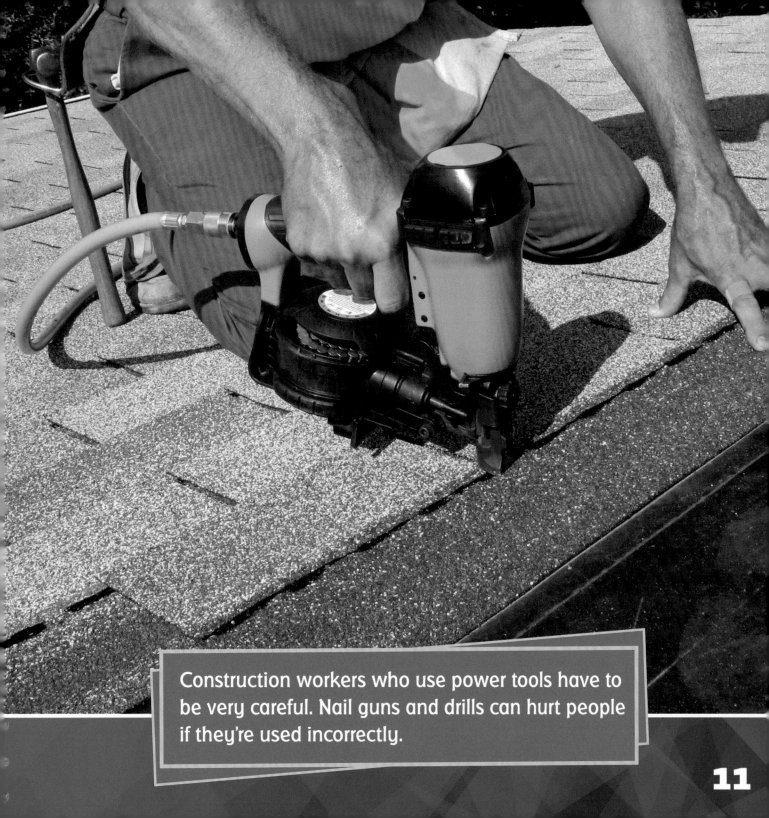

Construction workers who use power tools have to be very careful. Nail guns and drills can hurt people if they're used incorrectly.

Digging

Some construction workers have to dig in dirt on the construction site. They might need to break up dirt to make it easier to move. A pickax has a long handle and a head that's pointed on both sides. A construction worker can swing the pickax into the ground to break up dirt and other **materials**.

A construction worker might also use a shovel for digging. Shovels have a handle on one end and a flat blade on the other for **scooping**.

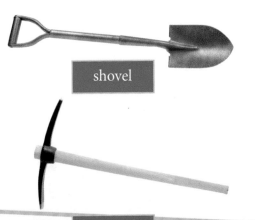

shovel

pickax

jackhammer

TOOL TIME!

Construction workers use jackhammers to break up hard surfaces, such as rock and concrete. A jackhammer is a power tool that drives a strong hammer into a surface very quickly.

Sometimes construction workers have to move a lot of dirt or rocks. In that case, they might need a big machine! An excavator is a big machine for scooping dirt and other things.

13

Measuring

Construction workers have to be very careful when making measurements. Correct measurements are important for a building to be steady and strong. To measure, construction workers use rulers, measuring tapes, and levels.

Rulers and yardsticks are sticks with measurements on them. Some rulers are in U.S. standard units, such as yards, feet, and inches. Others are in metric units, such as meters and centimeters. Rulers can also be used to help draw straight lines. Measuring tapes are more **flexible** and used to measure longer things.

measuring tape

ruler

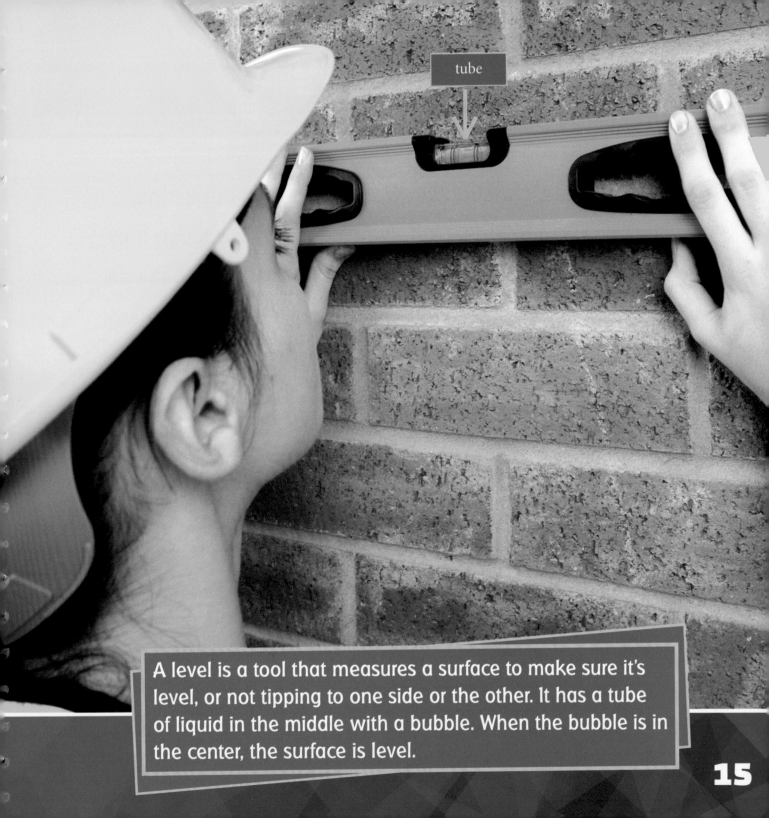

tube

A level is a tool that measures a surface to make sure it's level, or not tipping to one side or the other. It has a tube of liquid in the middle with a bubble. When the bubble is in the center, the surface is level.

15

Cutting

Sometimes, construction workers need to cut things, such as wooden boards. First, they measure how much they need. Then, they use a tool to cut the material. They can use a handsaw. Handsaws have a handle and a blade with many pointed teeth. A construction worker pushes the blade against the material to cut it.

Other saws are powered by electricity. Table saws can cut wooden boards quickly. They have a flat surface and a spinning circular saw.

chainsaw

handsaw

Chainsaws are handheld power tools that construction workers can use to cut down trees.

TOOL TIME!

Band saws have a thin metal band with sharp teeth. The band moves downward quickly to cut materials.

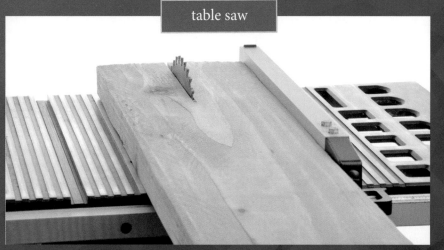

table saw

Reaching

Construction workers sometimes have to reach high places. They might be working on a tall **structure**, such as a skyscraper. It's important for construction workers to have tools to help them reach high areas.

Construction workers use ladders to reach things. Ladders have rungs, which are like thin stairs. Ladders can lean against a building or stand by themselves. Construction workers use scaffolding to reach higher places. Scaffolding is a **temporary** structure made of metal poles and beams.

boom lift

TOOL TIME!

Boom lifts are huge machines that lift workers to high places. They're also called cherry pickers or basket cranes.

Scaffolding is often used by construction workers who are building, cleaning, or fixing the outside of a building.

Big Tools

Construction workers use many small tools, but they use huge tools, too! Construction trucks and tractors do a lot of the heavy lifting, digging, and moving for construction workers. Some workers are skilled in driving these machines.

A crane is a huge machine that lifts heavy objects, moves them, and lowers them. Tower cranes can stretch very high. A dump truck is a truck with an open bed in the back. It can carry sand and dirt and then dump it in another place.

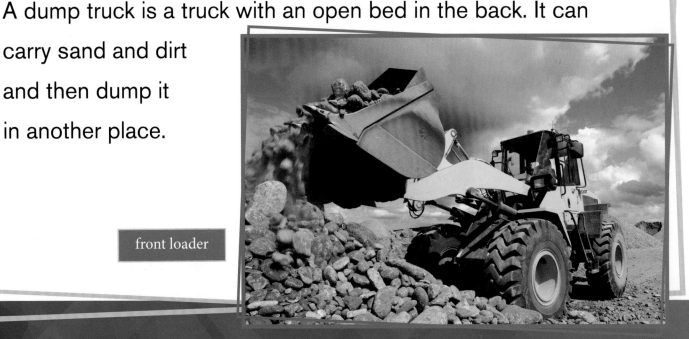

front loader

A Construction Worker's Tools

what to wear

hard hat

bright vest

tool belt

boots

small tools

hammer

screwdriver

power tools

nail gun

drill

big tools

crane

front loader

dump truck

bulldozer

measuring

ruler

measuring tape

level

cutting

handsaw

table saw

band saw

reaching

ladder

scaffolding

boom lift

digging

excavator

shovel

jackhammer

pickax

Building a Community

Do you want to drive a dump truck someday? Do you like to use hammers and screwdrivers to build and fix things? You can practice using some small tools. Be careful, though. Safety is important in construction.

Next time you walk around your neighborhood, look at all the different structures around you. Each house, road, school, and bridge was made by a team of construction workers. The construction workers could not have done the job without the help of important tools!

Glossary

flexible: Able to bend easily.

material: Something that's made of matter. Something used to make something else.

protect: To keep safe.

scoop: To pick something up and move it.

site: A place where a building stands or where something is being built.

source: The cause or starting point of something.

structure: A building.

temporary: Lasting for a short amount of time.

visible: Able to be seen.

Index

B
band saws, 17, 21
boom lifts, 18, 21
boots, 6, 7, 21
bulldozer, 5, 21

C
chainsaws, 16
cranes, 4, 20, 21

D
drill, 10, 11, 21

E
excavator, 13, 21

F
front loader, 20, 21

H
hammers, 4, 8, 10, 12, 21, 22
handsaw, 16, 21
hard hats, 6, 21

J
jackhammer, 12, 21

L
ladders, 18, 21
level, 14, 15, 21

M
measuring tape, 14, 21

N
nail gun, 10, 11, 21

P
pickax, 12, 21

R
rulers, 14, 21

S
safety glasses, 6
scaffolding, 18, 19, 21
screwdrivers, 4, 8, 10, 21, 22
shovel, 12, 21

T
table saw, 16, 17, 21
tool belt, 9, 21
trucks, 4, 6, 20, 21

V
vests, 6, 21

Y
yardsticks, 14

Websites

Due to the changing nature of Internet links, PowerKids Press has developed an online list of websites related to the subject of this book. This site is updated regularly. Please use this link to access the list: www.powerkidslinks.com/cht/cons